Toward My Father's House

HOPE -FILLED MEDITATIONS FOR THE TERMINALLY ILL

Mary Jane Mason
1935-1992

One Liguori Drive, Liguori, MO 63057-9999

Dedication

To my wonderful husband and God-given family who wholeheartedly supported my decision to forgo chemotherapy.
To Father Steve Makranyi who helped me relate my decisions to the will of the Father.
Thank you.

Imprimi Potest:
Richard Thibodeau, C.Ss.R.
Provincial, Denver Province
The Redemptorists

ISBN 978-0-7648-0698-8

Printed in the United States of America
07 08 09 10 11 6 5 4 3

Liguori Lifespan is an imprint of Liguori Publications.

To order, call 1-800-325-9521
www.liguori.org

Cover design by Lynne Condellone

Introduction

When first diagnosed with a terminal illness, many thoughts and feelings filled me. *Thank you, Father, for the invitation to come home. Am I ready? Has my life been all that you expected of me?*

There were feelings of excitement at the thought of heaven. *How must I prepare? What must I do to enhance my spiritual life?* There were feelings of sadness at leaving those who are dear to me: my husband and children, relatives and friends.

Now I journey toward my Father's house. Throughout our lives, we listen to the Word of God and are comforted by his words in times of sorrow. We are instructed by Scripture and revelation on how to live so as to reach heaven and enjoy eternal peace and rest. Why are we so afraid to say "Yes" when we finally receive the invitation to come home?

For the past few months, I have experienced many phases of Christ's life on earth. I have come to know the unimportance of material things and what people think of me. I have grown to know and love the life of the Spirit. Praised be our loving Father, who cares for us so well!

Mary Jane Mason

Time

There is an appointed time for everything,
and a time for every affair under the heavens.
A time to be born, and a time to die....
A time to weep, and a time to laugh;
a time to mourn, and a time to dance...
a time to keep, and a time to cast away.

ECCLESIASTES 3:1-2,4,6

When God reveals to us that our time to leave this earth is approaching, we weep a little. Indeed, it is sad to think of leaving those we love. But we set those feelings aside and go on living each day we're given. We live, confident that God is holding our hand to help us through this distressing time.

We hold on to a sense of humor. We need to laugh at our disabilities, to humble ourselves. We recognize our total dependence on God for our very existence.

We mourn. Ultimately, however, we dance. We dance at the thrill of entering the kingdom. We rejoice that our time here is ending and we will soon enter our Father's house.

We recognize and value life's most precious gifts. We cast away all attachment to things of this world and strive to enter fully into the life of the Spirit.

If the Father has loved us so much as to give us the knowledge of impending death, then he surely will send his Spirit to guide us to him. We open our heart to receive his inspirations and understand that death is not to be feared. It is but the entrance to eternal life.

Powerlessness

"You would have no power over me if it had not been given to you from above."

JOHN 19:11

After accepting the fact that there is no cure, we are ready to accept God's divine plan for our future. We are ready to accept our own powerlessness and the powerlessness of others. If God loves us so much as to give us "fair warning," then we certainly owe God the courtesy of becoming one with him in living out his will each remaining minute of our life. For example, if a medication is going to affect our ability to be the loving person God designed, then we have the right to refuse that treatment.

Standing in the Sandals of Jesus

Because the medical professionals are primarily concerned with physical treatments, they often fail to understand the workings of the Spirit in a person preparing to enter eternal life. They often become as Pilate, feeling a sense of power over our lives. But their power comes from the divine Healer, and if it is not the Healer's will to heal, they will have no power whatsoever.

We stand in the sandals of Jesus and accept the Father's plan for us. We offer our sufferings, our very lives, that others might be brought to God for all eternity. One with God, we long to fulfill God's will. For he is a loving Father who wants to bring us home. We abandon ourselves to powerlessness—and into the hands of God.

Compassion

The LORD is with me; I am not afraid;
what can mortals do against me?
The LORD is with me as my helper;
I shall look in triumph on my foes.
Better to take refuge in the LORD
than to put one's trust in mortals.

PSALM 118:6-8

It's hard for the doctor to give us the news; it's hard for us to hear it. In this time of distress, we turn to our Father for help; we do not become angry with the doctor. We draw on God's ever-present grace as we try to accept the fact that it's time for us to leave this earth for a celestial dwelling place.

All of our lives we have heard about the glories of the heavenly kingdom. Yet, when faced with its realities, we begin to fear and lament.

The "Yellow Brick Road" That Leads Home

Now is the time to turn to our Creator and ask for the grace and strength we need to follow the "yellow brick road" that leads us to our Father's house.

Now is the time to pray for those who will medically care for us. Theirs is a difficult and helpless task, for they know they cannot offer us a cure. They need us—and we need them. They need our compassion as they struggle with their own helplessness—and we need their support in offering us whatever forms of relief are available.

Treatment

Make known to me your ways, LORD;
teach me your paths.
Guide me in your truth and teach me,
for you are God my savior.
For you I wait all the long day.

PSALM 25:4-5

Determining a course for treatment is for some a difficult decision; for others, there is never a doubt. How will our decision affect those who love us?

Trust these decisions into God's loving hands. Life is a series of sufferings and joys. And though there will be some period of suffering for all, God, in his mercy, will grant understanding and eventual peace.

Death is inevitable for each of us. Our acceptance and preparation for it brings us the inner peace we hoped for—for ourselves, our family, and our friends. We learn not to fear what others think, not to worry about things out of our control, not to fear suffering. Our merciful God grants us peace.

Choose to Love

Medical personnel seldom understand the workings of the Spirit. They conclude that our attitude is fatalistic. But fatalism is an anticipation of ruination and destruction. Acceptance, on the other hand, is receiving with approval and satisfaction. If we accept God's will, our attitude is truly healthy. We may choose to forgo treatment that may alter our physical and emotional behavior and make us unpleasant to be around. In making that decision, we choose to love; we choose to be the loving person we were created to be. If we wait patiently for our Savior, he will make known his ways to us, and our decision will be one with his.

Sadness

Let me alone, that I may recover a little
Before I go whence I shall not return,
to the land of darkness and of gloom.

JOB 10:20-21

When we receive the news that we have an incurable disease, numerous thoughts race through our mind: fear, anger, sadness, concern for others. As children of God, we turn to our heavenly Father for consolation and help.

There is sadness at the idea of leaving those we dearly love. Yet, we need not be concerned for the welfare of others. God will place comforting arms around them. Those who love us are left to serve God where they are needed. God will be their consolation and joy in this time of sadness.

He Will Walk With Us

Sadness is a natural part of life. Jesus was sad when he heard of Lazarus' death. He understands our feelings and will help us—and those we love—through the challenges ahead. He will walk with us daily, blessing us with a positive manner. And quietly, deep within, we know his love for us and his great plans for our eternal joy. The sadness remains—but is embraced in abiding peace.

Denial

When a maid saw [Peter] seated in the light, she looked intently at him and said, "This man too was with him." But he denied it saying, "Woman, I do not know him." A short while later someone else saw him and said, "You too are one of them"; but Peter answered, "My friend, I am not." About an hour later, still another insisted, "Assuredly, this man too was with him, for he also is a Galilean." But Peter said, "My friend, I do not know what you are talking about." Just as he was saying this, the cock crowed, and the Lord turned and looked at Peter; and Peter remembered the word of the Lord, how he had said to him, "Before the cock crows today, you will deny me three times." He went out and began to weep bitterly.

LUKE 22:56-62

Many experience a period of denial when they're informed of a terminal illness. "Not I," they insist.

It is difficult to admit that we are vulnerable to disease. We fear death and choose to deny its inevitability, just as Peter feared death and chose to deny his Lord and Savior. Once he saw the look that Jesus gave him, however, he deeply regretted his actions. He wept.

So, too, with us. When Jesus calls us to be with him, he doesn't want us to be afraid; he doesn't want us to deny him. He looks for us to lean on him for strength to bear the sufferings leading to our death. He looks for us to accept, not deny, his invitation to come home. He rewards us for our faithfulness to his Father's will. He offers us the spiritual help we need, never demanding more physical suffering than we are capable of bearing.

Living Life to Its Fullest

Our Father is extremely good; he gives us this advance knowledge and lets us have time to prepare for our heavenly homecoming. It is our privilege to accept his will. This does not mean that we "give up" living. No, we simply go on working to fulfill the divine plan, living life to its fullest. For we are a chosen lot. In his mercy, God lovingly gives us an advance invitation.

Fruit of the Spirit

The fruit of the Spirit is love, joy, peace, patience, kindness, generosity, faithfulness, gentleness, self-control....Those who belong to Christ [Jesus] have crucified their flesh with its passions and desires.

GALATIANS 5:22-23,24

We know God is fully present to us during this final stage of our life. Even if we have not been totally successful at mortifying our senses and desires through penance, God gives us this splendid opportunity to accept the failings of our physical existence. Through Christ, our suffering takes on meaning and redemptive power. We gradually become more aware of the workings of the Spirit within us.

Perhaps we had to memorize the fruit of the Holy Spirit years ago as we prepared to celebrate the sacrament of confirmation. Have we considered its significance in our lives since that time? Now, as we journey toward our Father's house, we see evidence of this fruit in our day-to-day living.

Love: We watch our family members, friends, and acquaintances reach out to us. We are deeply touched by their cards, calls, prayers, and visits. We see love in our midst. Even the "beautiful cowards," those who shy away because they're uncomfortable and don't know what to say or do, touch us with their distant caring. We can reach out to these caring people by sharing our thoughts and feelings, thus inviting them into our privileged experience. All the while, the Spirit enlarges our heart with love.

Joy: To know that we will soon be entering the front door of our Father's house, to know release from pain and suffering, to gaze upon the face of God, to mingle among the saints who have preceded us: this is joy!

Peace: As we come to accept our Father's will, as we succumb to the limitations of our body and recognize the necessity of our dependence on others, as we admit to our finiteness and realize our vulnerability, we are embraced with peace. This is the Spirit.

Patient endurance: When the suffering is unbearable, when those who care for us cannot answer every call as quickly as we wish, when the professionals say they can do nothing more to help us, when we see our friends and loved ones struggling with their own vulnerability: these are times when the Spirit's gift of patience settles in our heart.

Kindness and mildness: We're not able to physically contribute to the needs of others. Yet, the Spirit helps us respond with kindness and mildness to the supporting efforts of others. How much more tolerable their work becomes when our response is pleasant.

Faith: The closer we come to union with our Father, the greater our faith and trust in divine Providence. We become more childlike, just as Jesus tells us we must to enter heaven.

As we progress in our faith life, we see this fruit of the Spirit developing within us, around us. We realize more and more that it is, indeed, okay to die.

Bitterness

Tremble and do not sin;
upon your beds ponder in silence.

PSALM 4:5

Give up your anger, abandon your wrath;
do not be provoked; it brings only harm.

PSALM 37:8

Be angry but do not sin; do not let the sun set on your anger, and do not leave room for the devil....All bitterness, fury, anger, shouting, and reviling must be removed from you, along with all malice.

EPHESIANS 4:26-27,31

Self-pity drives us to ask,"Why me, Lord?" Perhaps it is our humanness, our natural inclination to survival. Yet, we gain nothing by nurturing anger. No one is an earth inhabitant forever. We each have our own time to be born and our own time to die.

What a privilege it is to be given a glimpse of our dying time. With grateful anticipation, we prepare for that glorious meeting with our Father. We rob ourselves of tremendous peace if we let anger and bitterness coat the precious time remaining to us.

Even Jesus, blameless and sinless, faced the terror of the cross without bitterness. He merited no punishment yet bore no anger toward his Father, his accusers, or his executioners. He responded with acceptance. He knew the role he played in salvation history, in the eternal life of you and me.

Our Own Gethsemane

We each go through our own Gethsemane, our own time of fear. And we are given the same opportunity Jesus had: to fall before our loving God and say, "Thy will be done."

It's especially easy to become angry and bitter with the medical professionals. Few of them understand our faith journey and thus may treat our choice to forgo treatment with some measure of disrespect. We must let go of our anger toward them and toward all those who do not understand the workings of the Spirit in the terminally ill. As we pray for those who "persecute" us, we find our anger turns to compassion. The Spirit never ceases to enlarge our heart with spiritual fruit.

Grief

Happy the man who meditates on wisdom,
and reflects on knowledge;
Who ponders her ways in his heart,
and understands her paths.

SIRACH 14:20-21

We have to understand what others are feeling during this time. Some people are uncomfortable talking about death or being around someone who is terminally ill. They care; they just don't know how to express their concern. We put everyone at ease by bringing up the subject of death ourselves, especially if we can do it with humor and a positive attitude.

A Positive Attitude

Those that love us are going to grieve deeply when they think ahead to our absence. If we keep our conversation on the positive side, however, we support them and boost their spirits. If a serious discussion about death and arrangements is warranted, our calm and positive participation helps keep reality in perspective. Acceptance of the facts becomes easier for everyone.

Be open and sensitive to the thoughts and feelings of others. They are grieving and need our help as they move toward acceptance. Remaining present to the feelings of others keeps us from falling into the depths of our own self-pity and despair.

Encouragement

Blessed be the God and Father of our Lord Jesus Christ, the Father of compassion and God of all encouragement, who encourages us in our every affliction, so that we may be able to encourage those who are in any affliction with the encouragement with which we ourselves are encouraged by God. For as Christ's sufferings overflow to us, so through Christ does our encouragement also overflow. If we are afflicted, it is for your encouragement and salvation; if we are encouraged, it is for your encouragement, which enables you to endure the same sufferings that we suffer. Our hope for you is firm, for we know that as you share in the sufferings, you also share in the encouragement.

2 Corinthians 1:3-7

If our families and friends are aware of our faith, they will know we are not really abandoning them as we prepare to enter our Father's house. Our presence and service on earth may be terminated, but our love and care for others will continue into eternity. For where we go, we want those we love to follow. We will continue to work and pray for them. In fact, from our Father's house, we may be a far greater help to others than we could ever be on earth.

The Ever-Present Love of the Father

God is a loving, caring Father who will not abandon us or others. As he always has and always will, God offers us the life of his grace and unconditional love.

It's hard for us to understand this right now. After all, we only know our own human reactions to pain, suffering, and loss. Ultimately, however, our Father's designs work for the best.

Let us rejoice and be glad! We journey toward our Father's house. We near the threshold of heaven. May our family and friends rejoice with us and come to experience the consolation of Jesus Christ.

Courage

You are not lacking in any spiritual gift as you wait for the revelation of our Lord Jesus Christ. He will keep you firm to the end, irreproachable on the day of our Lord Jesus [Christ].

1 Corinthians 1:7-8

When physical pain grips us, it's hard to be pleasant toward others. We easily drift into self-pity and become demanding. Yet, we are called upon, as Christ was, to bear these sufferings. He was most courageous, even though he knew the terrible agony he had to undergo. He remained the faithful Son, even during those last desolate hours when he felt totally forsaken by his friends and even his Father. He bore no malice toward anyone, willingly undergoing the terror of crucifixion and opening for us the doors to our Father's house. He set for us a human example: courage in the face of fear, pain, and death.

Jesus is present to us, here, now, to comfort us,

to give us the courage we need to bear these trials. He knows that great blessings await us—and he sincerely wants us to partake of them.

"Keep on Truckin'"

With effort on our part and grace on God's, we suffer silently. We replace a grimace with a laugh. We are a joy to be around. We give hope to the hopeless. We are for others what Jesus has been for us. We "keep on truckin'," even though it's difficult.

This courage, this faith, is of the Spirit. We are led along the journey, with all those who love and care for us, toward our Father's house.

Acceptance

Your kingdom come,
your will be done.

MATTHEW 6:10

It is a privilege to receive the God's invitation to come home. What joy to know that soon we will share in the everlasting life of peace and eternal happiness. Here on earth we cannot possibly comprehend the reality of that kind of happiness. We can speculate about such glory, but we cannot know it. Accepting the Father's invitation to come home and join him can bring great excitement.

Perhaps we've known and envied others who have known of their own impending death. They could prepare, both spiritually and practically, for that great event.

The Responsibilities of the Privileged

Now, we are among that privileged band. Ah, but the privileged carry a heavy responsibility. From this moment on, each day is a holy day, to be lived to the fullest. Each hour, each minute, must somehow prepare us for arrival at the threshold of our Father's house.

Realizing the depth of our sinfulness and aware of limited time, we throw ourselves on the mercy of the heavenly court. We plead with the divine Judge to show us mercy, to draw from the infinite benefits of his Son's redemption, and to benevolently grant us the delights of eternal life.

As we accept the will of our Father, we are shown the path. "Draw near to God, and he will draw near to you" (James 4:8).

Rejoicing

I rejoiced when they said to me,
"Let us go to the house of the Lord.*"*

Psalm 122:1

Rejoice? To many, this may seem an unusual response to impending death. Yet, we know death is inevitable. Why not rejoice? New life—eternal life—awaits us.

There is a story told of a young boy who spent a great deal of time with his grandfather; the two of them were very close. One day the lad asked the old gentleman if he ever saw God. After a long pause, Grandfather replied, "All the time!"

When we acknowledge the inevitability of our own death, we see God "all the time," in everyone and everything. In fact, we recognize God so often that we glow with anticipation. Soon we will behold our beloved Father face to face.

Rejoicing may seem like an unrealistic, perhaps disrespectful, response to terminal disease, especially to those who cling tenaciously to life and the things of this world. But to those who know God, rejoicing is the only way to accept the invitation!

Our Very Best Finery

When we're invited to attend a celebration, we accept with gladness and anticipation. We concentrate on being our very best: acting our best and wearing our very best finery.

Our Father's invitation to come home is the greatest invitation we'll ever receive. We prepare with all of our being to become a more fitting guest of our heavenly Host. Let us rejoice and be glad!

Darkness

How long, LORD? Will you utterly forget me?
How long will you hide your face from me?
How long must I carry sorrow in my soul,
grief in my heart day after day?
How long will my enemy triumph over me?

Look upon me, answer me, LORD, my God!
Give light to my eyes lest I sleep in death,
Lest my enemy say, "I have prevailed,"
lest my foes rejoice at my downfall.

I trust in your faithfulness.
Grant my heart joy in your help,
That I may sing of the LORD,
"How good our God has been to me!"

PSALM 13:2-6

No matter how strong our faith, we will occasionally feel ourselves adrift in darkness. When the pain overwhelms us, we wonder if God is really a God of love. We question his care. We feel alone. In the midst of this darkness, we cry out, "Look at me, Lord! Answer me!" The silence that echoes back intensifies the darkness.

Do not fear the darkness; God is at work. We are being prepared for the glory that is soon to be ours. Saint John of the Cross, Saint Teresa of Avila, and all the great saints and Doctors of the Church have experienced this dark night of the soul. They have taught us that the dark night prepares us to receive great things from our God, to realize the fullness of glory that he does, indeed, have waiting for us.

The Gift of Inner Peace

Some of us will never "feel" anything supernatural in this life on earth. Yet, if we remain faithful through these dark times, inner peace is God's gift to us now. The knowledge that God cares will be instilled inside us; that is his gift of understanding. We rest with assurance that he is reserving much, much more for us in heaven!

Depression

Be patient, therefore,...until the coming of the Lord....Take as an example of hardship and patience,...the prophets who spoke in the name of the Lord.

JAMES 5:7,10

It is difficult to be patient and cheerful when our suffering is prolonged. Yet, our suffering plays a significant role in our journey toward our Father's house. Although God seems silent and distant, he knows the depths of our suffering and is close, closer than we perceive. The pain and God's seeming distance are part of our preparation for eternal glory.

A Model Who Made It Home

We look around for models. Scripture, for example, offers us the perseverance of the prophets; the lives of the saints celebrate the virtues of patient faith. Usually, we can find someone to use as our mentor, someone who has "made it home."

When depression comes knocking at our door, we can refuse it entry. We can busy ourselves by reaching out to others, by doing what we can physically, and by focusing on prayer. We can listen to inspirational songs that lift our mind and heart to God. We can read the lives of the saints and learn their art of being pleasant and cheerful.

It is dispiriting and emotionally degrading to be around someone who is forever depressed. Saint Teresa of Avila reminded her sisters that God doesn't want "gloomy saints." Surprisingly—or maybe not so surprisingly—we feel better in the company of others who are cheerful, who respond with lighthearted humor, who laugh with us. We are happier, feel better about ourselves, and allow others to understand the great rewards of a faith-filled life when we set our depression aside and walk through our days with confidence and anticipation.

Mortality

"Naked I came forth from my mother's womb,
and naked shall I go back again.
The LORD *gave and the* LORD *has taken away;*
blessed be the name of the LORD*!"*

JOB 1:21

As we approach the threshold to our new life, and the reality of our own mortality is reflected back to us from the mirror every day, we begin to realize our total dependence on the Father. We notice that everything we need does, indeed, come from God. We learn that God is aware of all our needs and enfolds us in grace during our times of distress and trouble. Even though we do not have all that we want, we certainly have all that we need.

Thy Will; My Will

"Thy will be done..." "My will be done...". From the depths of our human limitations, we utter both these prayers. Yet, as we look back over the years, we can see that God's will *is* done, and always for our best interest.

More and more, God helps us understand what is needed to be born to new life. Physically, we leave this earth as we arrived: naked. Yet, we trust that the treasure chest of our soul is full of a greater knowledge of the Father and his future plans for us. As we can release life into the hands of our loving Father, he clothes us in our spiritual garments and escorts us toward his house.

Weakness

He said to me, "My grace is sufficient for you, for power is made perfect in weakness." I will rather boast most gladly of my weaknesses, in order that the power of Christ may dwell with me. Therefore, I am content with weaknesses, insults, hardships, persecutions, and constraints, for the sake of Christ; for when I am weak, then I am strong.

2 Corinthians 12:9-10

As we learn to live with our disabilities and bodily weaknesses, Saint Paul's words to the people in Corinth take on a deeper meaning. We learn to laugh at our incompetence and understand our weaknesses. We become more forgiving of others and more resigned to God's will. We become increasingly dependent on God for our strength in times of distress.

That is what Paul is trying to tell us. Amazing spiritual strength is ours when we recognize and admit our weaknesses and call upon God to assist us. We cease to focus on our own strengths; we let go of control. And in that space of weakness, we are made strong as the power of Christ dwells in us.

Physical Weaknesses; Spiritual Giants

Physical weakness produces spiritual giants because time becomes a crucial factor. Along the way to our Father's house, we have the time to meditate on God, on his providence. Time is a gift to us. We value its importance and use it well to conquer our physical and spiritual shortcomings.

We become more and more prepared to walk with our Father toward his house. We become more and more dependent on him as we realize his abundant grace in each moment of weakness.

Trust

Praise the LORD, my soul;
I shall praise the LORD all my life,
sing praise to my God while I live.

Put no trust in princes,
in mere mortals powerless to save.
When they breathe their last,
they return to the earth;
that day all their planning comes to nothing.
Happy those whose help is Jacob's God,
whose hope is in the LORD, *their God,*
The maker of heaven and earth,
the seas and all that is in them,
Who keeps faith forever,
secures justice for the oppressed,
gives food to the hungry.
The LORD *sets prisoners free;*
the LORD *gives sight to the blind.*
The LORD *raises up those*
who are bowed down;
the LORD *loves the righteous.*
The LORD *protects the stranger,*
sustains the orphan and the widow,
but thwarts the way of the wicked.
The LORD *shall reign forever,*
your God, Zion, through all generations!
Hallelujah!

PSALM 146

As our body begins to fail us, we learn to trust God. Ultimately, he is in command of our living and dying. We have exercised our free will throughout our lifetime, but when it comes to birth and death, God alone holds the reins. We trust that he will show us how to suffer, that he will hold up for us the model of his Son, Jesus Christ. We trust that he will fill us with the same joy the shepherds and angels knew at his birth; that he will show us how to be cheerful in our trials, just as the saints were, and will care for those who are left behind. We trust that he will show his mercy toward us regarding our past indiscretions.

Our Father Leads the Way

We trust that God will share the glories of his heavenly house with us when we leave this earth.

We trust our Father with our every physical, emotional, and spiritual need. Left to ourselves, we can do nothing. But with our Father leading the way, we can do all that he wills us to accomplish in the time we have remaining on earth.

Faith

"Do not let your hearts be troubled. You have faith in God; have faith also in me. In my Father's house there are many dwelling places. If there were not, would I have told you that I am going to prepare a place for you? And if I

go and prepare a place for you, I will come back again and take you to myself, so that where I am you also may be."

JOHN 14:1-3

Jesus promised to "prepare a place" for his disciples. All of our life, this divine promise has sustained us. This is what has kept us living and working for the Lord as we serve others.

Now, as we humbly allow others to serve us in our weaknesses, we need to keep this promise close at heart. When we're not feeling well physically, it's a chore to be cheerful; it's hard to be appreciative of what others do for us. Holding this promise close at heart, however, strengthens our faith. We know the gaze of our Father as he holds us steadily in his sight. We feel his strength arming us with faith.

We Cling to the Promise

Our Father is coming to take us home with him. Jesus promised. We cling to that promise with certainty; we rely on faith, and we long for the peace of our eternal home.

Loneliness

Then he said to [the disciples], "My soul is sorrowful even to death. Remain here and keep watch." He advanced a little and fell to the ground and prayed that if it were possible the hour might pass by him; he said, "Abba, Father, all things are possible to you. Take this cup away from me, but not what I will but what you will." When he returned he found them asleep.

MARK 14:34-37

Dying is a lonely journey. No one really understands except those who have gone before us: the saints. Because they have experienced all phases of death and dying, they will intercede for us in our hour of need.

We are grateful for those who try to be compassionate and understanding during this time. We appreciate their loving and tireless efforts. They are giving us their best. But they cannot be present to us all the time; they cannot meet our every need. They have their own lives and other obligations. Our response is to feel alone.

God's only Son experienced the loneliness and emptiness of dying. As he hung on the cross, he cried,

"My God, my God, why have you forsaken me?" (Mark 15:34).

Part of the Scenery on the Way Home

When we feel the depths of loneliness descending upon us, we can unite our mind and heart with our divine Redeemer. Our aloneness allows us to share in his passion, loneliness, and death. He knew—and we know—that loneliness is part of the scenery along the journey toward our Father's house. He knew—and we know—that the homecoming awaiting us is no less joyful, no less splendid.

Hope

Beloved, we are God's children now; what we shall be has not yet been revealed. We do know that when it is revealed we shall be like him, for we shall see him as he is. Everyone who has this hope based on him makes himself pure, as he is pure.

1 John 3:2-3

There is an element of excitement to our dying journey. It's like a child going to the circus for the first time. The youngster doesn't know what it's really going to be like but hopes that, indeed, it is the "greatest show on earth." For us, arrival at our

Father's house will be the greatest show we can experience beyond the confines of this earth.

With simple childlikeness, we wonder about eternal life. What will it be like? From what we've been taught, eternity will far exceed our greatest expectations. It will be well worth working for, waiting for, praying for. It will be the realization of all our hopes and dreams. It will be an end to our pain and suffering. We will see the loving face of God.

Our Final Destination

To attain the fulfillment of this hope, to reach this goal of a lifetime, we continue each day to perfect our spiritual life. In hope, we travel the byroad of death to reach our final destination. If we persevere in our determination to serve God and others, our hope will blossom, even in our incapacity.

Purification

Do not grow slack in zeal, be fervent in spirit, serve the Lord. Rejoice in hope, endure in affliction, persevere in prayer....Bless those who persecute [you]....Rejoice with those who rejoice, weep with those who weep. Have the same regard for one another; do not be haughty but associate with the lowly; do not be wise in your own estimation. Do not repay anyone evil for evil; be concerned for what is noble in the sight of all....Beloved, do not look for revenge but leave room for the wrath....Do not be conquered by evil but conquer evil with good.

ROMANS 12:11-12,14,15-17,19,21

Paul's challenge to the Romans seems like a tremendous order, especially when our health is failing. We don't feel strong enough to do even one of these things, much less all of them. Yet, the weaker our body becomes, the stronger our spirit becomes. We are purified of all weaknesses. We become strong in the ways of the Lord. Without this process of purification, we cannot receive the favor of the Lord.

The closer we draw toward our Father's house, the more we need to be fortified in the ways of Christ. The purification of our spirit opens us to receive the mercy of the Father as we enter his vast eternity.

The Fruit of Purification

No, we can no longer perform great works. But we can become spiritual giants. We can lavish the very love of God on those who minister to and support us: family, friends, acquaintances, and medical personnel. It is in this purification that we conquer physical and emotional evil with good attitudes and warm responses. We grow in love of Jesus and learn to love as he loves. This is the fruit of purification.

Reflection

Teach us to count our days aright,
that we may gain wisdom of heart.
Relent, O LORD! How long?
Have pity on your servants!
Fill us at daybreak with your love,
that all our days we may sing for joy.
Make us glad as many days
as you humbled us,
for as many years as we have seen trouble.
Show your deeds to your servants,
your glory to their children.
May the favor of the Lord our God be ours.
Prosper the work of our hands!
Prosper the work of our hands!

PSALM 90:12-17

Afflicted with this terminal illness and aware of the brief and precious time left, we reflect on our past life. We wonder if we're ready to approach our heavenly Father.

Have we been all that he willed us to be? Have we made a sincere effort to serve him? Has our lifestyle been a good example for our children? Have we led others to know and serve the Lord? We reminisce; we have regrets.

Begin Anew

Fortunately, it's never too late to repent, never too late to begin anew. We never stop trying, for the Lord is truly merciful in his care for us.

The attitudes we develop concerning our illness and dying will be the attitudes our family remembers. If our disposition is positive and faith-filled, then the work of our hands will prosper in the eyes of the Lord. Our reflection, honest and blessed, will focus on both our strengths and our weaknesses, our goodness and our failures. Most of all, our reflection will put the present in perspective.

The journey toward our Father's house begins today. From this moment on, we treasure the favorable memories as we convey hope to our children. They, too, will journey this way.

Grace

The Lord watches over the way of the just.

Psalm 1:6

Sometimes we sit in wonder at the grace and patience of the Lord. Again and again, we fail with our own efforts; we turn away from the prompting of the Spirit. Yet, our Father never ceases to shower us with grace. He forgives our shortcomings and our failures, forever calling us back to himself.

We stubbornly cling to the ways of the world. And all the while, God smiles on us, offers us the grace to see things his way. He is steady and ever-present, always waiting. When the going gets rough for us, he reaches toward us with safe arms. We can choose to move into the safe harbor of his arms or shrink back.

Succumbing to Love

God gives us the freedom to make our own decisions, waiting patiently and lovingly, for us to respond to his grace and return our gaze to him. How much easier life becomes, how much more comfortable we feel, how peaceful our inner self can be when we finally begin to trust God, to see things his way, to succumb to Love.

The transition to eternity is beautiful, easy, and "grace-full" when we work with our hand in his. If we let God's grace enter our soul now, we will tread the path toward our Father's house with our soul ablaze with hope.

Longing

O God, you are my God—
for you I long!
For you my body yearns;
for you my soul thirsts,
Like a land parched, lifeless,
and without water.
So I look to you in the sanctuary
to see your power and glory.
For your love is better than life;
my lips offer you worship!

I will bless you as long as I live;
I will lift up my hands,
calling on your name.
My soul shall savor the rich banquet of praise,
with joyous lips
my mouth shall honor you!
When I think of you upon my bed,
through the night watches I will recall

That you indeed are my help,
and in the shadow of your wings
I shout for joy.
My soul clings fast to you;
your right hand upholds me.

PSALM 63:2-9

A longing for eternal life fills our soul—and it is good. Our heart is stretched, and we learn to rest peacefully in the longing for our heavenly home. Once again the Spirit is at work in our life, drawing us to the Father who created us, who also longs to have us return home to him.

When this longing for eternal rest overwhelms us, the "things" of earth diminish. Nothing seems important anymore except pleasing the Lord and doing his will. We long with hope to be released from the ties that bind us here. As the longing intensifies, the ties are loosed. We will soon have the freedom to soar to the heights of heaven and experience the glory of eternal life.

A Radiant Smile

It is good to meditate on this radiant experience. It helps us keep a smile on our face when we take our last earthly breath and inhale the celestial oxygen of eternal life.

Strength

I love you, Lord, my strength,
Lord, my rock, my fortress, my deliverer,
My God, my rock of refuge,
my shield, my saving horn, my stronghold!
Praised be the Lord, I exclaim!
I have been delivered from my enemies.

Psalm 18:2-4

Our spiritual strength begins when we are at our weakest, when we realize our finitude, when we face our own total helplessness. We call upon our God, and he gives us his own strength. He takes over and fills our every real need with the strength of saints. We feel the grip of death lose its power to cause fear—and we know the strength and peace of God.

When we feel ourselves slip into self-pity and depression, we call out to God. He gently picks us up, cradles us in the palm of his hand, and blesses us with strength, knowledge, and wisdom. We are able to handle the present situation with tremendous spiritual insight. We grow calm, serene, and peaceful, resting helpless in God's embrace. We are made stronger because we are made weaker.

A Single Set of Footprints

The "single set of footprints in the sand" are, indeed, the Lord's. He carries us in his great strong arms, and his strength becomes our strength. Our loving Father is generous in sharing with us his powerful strength of Spirit.

Sacrifice

I urge you therefore...by the mercies of God, to offer your bodies as a living sacrifice, holy and pleasing to God, your spiritual worship. Do not conform yourself to this age but be transformed by the renewal of your mind, that you may discern what is the will of God, what is good and pleasing and perfect.

ROMANS 12:1-2

The Father demanded the sacrifice of his Son's body on the cross. For us, that means eternal life. God asks the same total sacrifice of us. Jesus was humiliated and mocked, stripped of his garments, abandoned by his followers. Our sacrifice will entail the same. We will know humiliation as we watch physical limitations gaining a foothold. We will be stripped of our garments to undergo vast medical studies. We will be forgotten by acquaintances.

Jesus endured the cruel scourging at the pillar, the painful crowning of thorns, the unbearable weight of the cross, and the agonizing pain of crucifixion. We unite our scourgings, our thorns, our crosses, and our crucifixion with his suffering—and we are rewarded with the fruit of redemption.

The autumn leaves dance with brilliant colors as they enter their final stage of life. They dance, they fall, and they move on. The cycle is imminent, always bursting forth with new life at the appointed time.

The Winter of Dying —The Springtime of Birth

Our life is like the autumn leaves: we take on new beauty in our sacrifice. The autumn of life—this journey toward our Father's house—prepares us for the winter of dying and the springtime of birth. The ultimate reward for the sacrifices we offer is eternal joy.

Peace

We do not cease praying for you and asking that you may be filled with the knowledge of his will through all spiritual wisdom and understanding to live in a manner worthy of the Lord, so as to be fully pleasing, in every good work bearing fruit and growing in the knowledge of God, strengthened with every power, in accord with his glorious might, for all endurance and patience, with joy giving thanks to the Father, who has made you fit to share in the inheritance of the holy ones in light.

COLOSSIANS 1:9-12

"We're praying for you." What peace, to know that there are prayers assisting the healing of our body and spirit. As our physical health deteriorates and we become weaker, our soul becomes stronger. Our spirit becomes enlightened with the wisdom of God—and a quiet interior peace settles in the center of our soul. Death is not frightening, but longed for. Charity is no longer difficult, but a natural joy. Suffering is no longer debilitating, but a source of strength and peace.

When these virtues become stronger, the way of the Lord becomes easier. We long to be numbered among the saints in heaven who knew no greater joy than serving their Creator. They looked upon death as a glorious event. The closer we draw to our heavenly Father, the more we, too, will look forward to this exciting meeting.

For Now...

For now, we live in peace, a peace that is merely a foretaste of the eternal peace of our Father's house.

Eternity

I consider that the sufferings of this present time are as nothing compared with the glory to be revealed for us. For creation awaits with eager expectation the revelation of the children of God; for creation was made subject to futility, not of its own accord but because of the one who subjected it, in hope that creation itself would be set free from slavery to corruption and share in the glorious freedom of the children of God.

Romans 8:18-21

Saint Paul speaks of our weak human condition and the corruption of our bodies. We know that we return to the earth, that every human being must ultimately deal with mortality. However, our heart has grown strong. As we have studied the truths that Christ left for us, our spirit has expanded with hope for a splendid eternity.

Jesus taught us this. The gospel writers have captured this truth in the Scriptures, and the saints have reconfirmed it by their lives of faith and service. We know eternity is ours, and we long for its fulfillment.

A Glimpse of the Glory

Watch. When we know we are working for the Lord and journeying toward eternity, our actions and attitudes radiate a positive anticipation. We are going home. We marvel at the splendor of sunshine, the fragrance of blossoms, the change of the seasons, and the complexity of birth. We know that such wondrousness is but a glimpse of the glories that await us in eternity.

Enlightenment

...that the God of our Lord Jesus Christ, the Father of glory, may give you a spirit of wisdom and revelation resulting in knowledge of him. May the eyes of [your] hearts be enlightened, that you may know what is the hope that belongs to his call, what are the riches of glory in his inheritance among the holy ones, and what is the surpassing greatness of his power for us who believe.

Ephesians 1:17-19

As our days on this earth grow visibly numbered, this message of Saint Paul comes alive in our mind and heart. This is enlightenment, the life of the Holy

Spirit, uniting our every thought and action to that of the Father. Enlightenment intensifies our longing for both eternity and the arms of our Father.

Our every thought is God-centered, and every act is weighed upon the scale of divine acceptance. Nothing seems important except to please him who created us. The time remaining becomes a time of holy waiting, when the eyes of our heart are enlightened.

Eternity Touching Today

Our heavenly Father so desires our enlightenment that he sent his only Son to suffer and die that we might see the glory of eternity touching our daily lives. How imperative it is that we strive unceasingly to attain it.

Homecoming

As the deer longs for streams of water,
so my soul longs for you, O God.
My being thirsts for God, the living God.
When can I go and see the face of God?
Why are you downcast, my soul;
why do you groan within me?
Wait for God, whom I shall praise again,
my savior and my God.

PSALM 42—43:2-3,6

The more we turn our lives toward the fulfillment of God's plan for us, the more we seek to draw closer to him, to know him, to love him. The transition from this life to the next will be easy as long as God is leading us. What joy! Our homecoming is in the hands of God. He leads the way, *is* the Way—and the final Destination—and he will be there to greet us.

We cannot remain on earth forever. Yet, despite the pain, suffering, and limitations of this life, we foolishly cling to it. We attach ourselves to the empty securities of this world. How much better, to anticipate our glorious homecoming, to work toward and plan for it.

When we see our own death as our personal invitation to come home to the Father, we no longer fear. We walk through the threshold that separates this world from our Father's house, and we are home. A life of love, joy, and peace is ours.

Until Then...

Until that glorious moment arrives, however, we have the living memorial of Christ's passion to sustain us. We have Scripture, worship, Eucharist, and community as strength for daily living. May we immerse ourselves in the Christ in our midst with reverence, awe, and great hope! This is his way of sustaining us until the day of our homecoming.